HE PICKED UP THE PIECES

Copyright © 2018 by Durand L. Blackett

Edited by Durand L. Blackett

Book Cover Artwork by Durand L. Blackett

ISBN: 978-976-96205-0-6

ISBN: 978-976-96205-1-3 (e-book)

All rights reserved. No part of this publication may be reproduced or transmitted in any form or by any means, electronic or mechanical, including photocopy, recording, or any information storage and retrieval system, without permission in writing from the publisher.

Printed in the United States of America

Chapter 1.

Shattered

He can't remember the exact moment it happened. He recalls sitting in a dark, quiet room – thoughts thrown everywhere. Knowing where he was but he couldn't shake the feeling of being so lost. The ticking of the clock that hung on the wall was background noise. Don't ask him the time. He couldn't tell you even if he wanted to. Then, in a seemingly unprovoked instant he heard it, the loud sound of the cracking of his heart. It wasn't fractured, it was broken. The pieces fell within him. The bleeding was internal. The pain was unimaginable.

Her Letters.

I don't read your letters anymore
The words you wrote
The poems you quote
Our relationship became
A dark shade of gray
Finally I woke up
Realized I couldn't stay

Words on the pages
The flame for you
No longer rages
We've been through
Countless Stages

I'll throw them in the fire
I no longer possess the desire
Today I'm brave enough to aspire
For something real
Something higher

I Feel You.

The pain that you feel
I am sensitive to

The tears you refuse to cry
The screams you swallow
The self-hate you mask
The anger you bury
The guilt you conceal
The low self-esteem
You won't reveal
The crushing in your chest
That you insist
Doesn't exist

The pain that you feel
I am sensitive to
Yes I do
Truthfully
I feel you

He Has To.

Running so fast
The light around
Blurred into streaks
Air suffocates him
Yet he runs
Feet barely touching
The ground
He runs
Because he has to
Escape the darkness
That remains
On his heels

Don't Cry.

He has been hurting
For quite a while
Society told him

Ssssssshhhhhhh

Remain silent
Real men don't cry
Don't speak about
Your feelings
The reeling inside

This kind of pain
The reason why
Many before have died

He is not okay
But still he lies
Lies because
Real men don't cry

But this hurt
Isn't ordinary
Demanding to be seen
It claws its way out
Breaking through
The screen

Because years ago
Something in him fell
Smashed to the ground
But he wasn't allowed
To hurt out loud

Mental illness...

He hated that expression
It made him feel crazy
Like he was out of his mind
He hated that expression
It highlighted that something was wrong
That he wasn't well
Call the doctors
Put him in a straitjacket
Everyone he knows, knows
They are talking about him
Saying things like

"I always knew that something was off about him."

All this flashes before him
In his mind, in his mind only
This depression thing is lonely
All he came back to
Is the fact that he hated that expression
Mental illness...
It made him feel crazy
Or just maybe he hated it
Because he was hiding in the night
And it was high time
He stepped out into the light

Known As...

Imagine for a moment being set afire
Trapped in a transparent glass room
The walls slowly closing in
You see the world
Outside around you
People walking by
But they can't see you
As your skin burns
You scream at the top of your lungs
No one hears you

Welcome to the condition
Known as Depression.

The Privilege of Pain.

Even in the depths
Of his despair
His chest was still bursting
With endless gratitude
Because no matter what
It is a gift
To feel something
Anything

Sacred Tears.

The salt water that falls
From his eyes
Drop into the sea
Of his own despair

Wrong For Each Other.

Sometimes we hurt ourselves
Forcing it to work

But it never will

No matter how hard we pray
We will it to come together

But it never does

Because we are just two people
Who couldn't be more different
Just two mixed-matched pieces
Of a puzzle

Mother's foresight.

She foresaw the danger
Of a precious heart
Placed in the hands of a stranger

Mid-night Prayers.

Hands clasped tight
Eyes closed
He speaks
Like whispers
His prayers
Are confessions
The confrontation
Of his pain
Intentionally breaking
The chains
Disrupting sorrows reign
Making a sacred covenant
As the sweat rolls
Down his forehead

The Left Side.

The class room divided in two

On the right the fast learners
On the left the slow

He fell on the wrong side
Of the room
And so no matter

What he did

Or how well he did it

He will always remember
That he belongs

On the left side

Dearly Beloved.

Rose petals fall
The music plays
Echoes through the hall
Speeches being given
In the presence
Of the living

How do you find the words
To speak so eloquently
When I'm finding it hard
Just to breathe

Missing Her.

She was gone from him
Like a sweet distant dream

She faded

Leaving him more
Than slightly jaded

Guilty.

I suppose
We are all guilty
Of continually
Punishing ourselves
For mistakes
That we have
Already paid for
A hundred times over

Beautiful Hearts.

All the most beautiful hearts
Have been broken
Once or twice

The Weight.

He remembers those days
Waking up feeling so drained
'Get out of bed and face the day'
His mother would say
Unable to pull the strength from within
He doesn't know where to begin
A stone resides on his chest

Without a sound
It weighs him down

Gradually growing bigger
Every day getting heavier

Like all of his emotions, doubts and mistakes
Crushing him painfully, slowly
His energy it takes

Begin Somewhere.

Start by
Trying
To think
Highly
Of
Yourself

Broken Things Breaking Things.

> His bones broke
> Under the weight
> Of his broken heart

Depression.

It is a large snake coiling around your body. With every breath you take it tightens its grip, breaking your bones, squeezing the air from your lungs. The day is dark. Every day is dark, as the Sun's light no longer pierces the thick gloomy clouds. You try screaming but with no breath, no air to carry your voice, only silence fills this space. It is in this moment, as power abandons your very being, that you pray, you pray for relief, in any way, in any form, from your grief.

The Way it is.

In his dream
He was submerged
In a large body of water
He couldn't breathe
But he didn't die
He couldn't die
Surrounded by
A sheet of dark blue

He shivers
But there is no pain here
Residing beneath
A sheet of ice
Looking up he sees
People above
He drowns
As life goes on

Unheard.

His heart was wounded
Feelings flowing out in word
Perhaps the most painful thing
Was not being heard

He Waits.

He stands alone with white roses in hand
The sun rises slowly as he waits for her
Its warm light kisses his skin
As he eagerly anticipates the sight of her face
She promised she would be there
He holds those words close to his heart
As his love for her blooms

It's the late afternoon
He stands alone holding tightly
The white roses
A symbol of his love
He exposes
His heart
The sun burns it
It's getting late
Scorched skin as he waits

The sun finally descends
He can't stop his body from shaking
As the rain pours down
Rose petals fall to the ground
What once bloomed within his heart
Withered as he waited for her
She promised she would be there
Now he sees clearly

That she never really cared

We All Break.

It's never just one thing
That breaks the dam is it?
The constant pressure of the water
Cracks that appear over time

It wears down
Wears out

Eventually the dam will break
The water will rush through

Eventually we all break

Never Forget.

Part of the problem is
He allowed the world
To punch him with amnesia
He forgot many things
About himself
The fact that the good
Was greater than the bad
That his strengths
Outweighed his weaknesses
He forgot that
His light shines so bright
That it diminishes
The darkness
That he sometimes feels

Part of the problem is
He forgot who he was
He forgot what he was

Love is... Part 1.

His words may be beautiful
But remember that love is more than words
Love is so much more than words

Numb.

We have all been there before
Overwhelmed, bombarded by emotions
Clawing their way back to the surface
Loss in the wilderness, finding our purpose
Trapped within ourselves
Standing in a glass box

Mere observers
Of our own lives
Perfect pretenders
Looking out
At the world
Through our own eyes

Forced to unplug and disconnect
A version of ourselves interacting
Loudly laughing
Eloquently talking
These feelings passing

'It's better to be safe
Than to be happy'
Is what we say
The homes built within
Is where we'll stay

I Am Here.

I could be invisible
To the entire world

All I care about
Is that you
And only you
See me.

Life Lesson 1.

Listen. Just listen to the person standing
Or sitting in front of you
The one sinking in a sea of unspeakable
Overwhelming pain
Fight the urge to speak, to offer wise words
Let them pour out their hearts and bear their soul
Allow the river of their being to flow freely
Without diversion or interruption
Give them the opportunity to unburden themselves
The weight that they carry day after day as they struggle
To find words to make sense of the immense storm within
Sometimes all we need is a listening ear and a dry shoulder
Be there for the broken ones, be there and listen

Chapter 2.

Picking Up The Pieces.

He began making peace with his regrets. Life has no time machines. There is no going back. There is only learning, growing, progressing. So he took stock of his life. Counted his scars and interpreted their meaning. His mistakes were now his teacher. He thought of how his life could have been so different if only he knew better. If he knew what love really meant and was ready for it. Now here he is. A student in a class built by all of his grief. Picking up the pieces, he has never been more attentive then in this moment.

The Center.

In the center of our despair

We see no end in sight

It's easy to become enslaved to emotion

But if we are patient

If we are still, in the eye of the storm

I promise you, we will eventually return to ourselves

We will starve our fears

The reason for our trails

Will finally become clear

Culture of Silence.

I am afraid that if the culture
Insists that we do not speak
Of the things that are tearing us apart

For our own sake
We must exist outside of that culture.

Mortality.

It is in our quietest moments that we think
Falling deep within ourselves
Searching for answers
The reasons why we are
The way we are
The decisions we made
The mistakes we pay for

And in gathering the fragments
Left behind from this internal war
We silently come back
To the fact
That we are human
Flawed and beautiful creatures
Scarred
Such beautiful features

Please dear
Know that the memory of you
Will be bitter-sweet
Happy that you were here
Sad that you had to go

It Is Sacred...

If it is sacred

Let it be

Let it stand

In its own light

In its own glory

During the day

We admire its beauty

Under the sun's rays

At night

It engages our thoughts

Invades our dreams

If it is sacred

Let it be

Don't tarnish it

With your hands

Resist the urge

The mad obsession

To possess everything

That captures your attention

Learn to appreciate

Beautiful things

From a distance

Learn to allow

Precious things

To be free

A Mother's Love.

There from the beginning

Hand on her cheek

As I fall asleep

Stories from my youth

Waking her up at midnight

For warm tea

She turned on the light

So I could see

Eventually all boys become men

Strong and independent

On ourselves we depend

Tigers

Pray on the proud

Daggers

Lay on my chest

I retreat to her by request

She opens my hearts window

She lets in loves air

Love is a blend of blue and red

Present in everything she did

Everything she said

A mother's love is pure

Her love is sure

A mother's love

Is always the cure

12:45.

About quarter to one
It's all said and done
He gets down on his knees
Closing his eyes tight
Begging God to hear his pleas
His pain has a voice
Emerging from within
He no longer has a choice
Words pouring out
As he confesses
All of his pain and his doubts

The Apology.

He mustered the courage
To apologize to his heart
He didn't need to get burned
To know that fire was hot

My Father Would Say.

"Your present suffering
Is training"
He would say
"For whatever the future might bring"

Change.

Change is both
An uncomfortable
And necessary
Thing

For Them.

Tears dried on his cheek

Scars still visible on his back

His eyes no longer dazed

But focused on others

Those who are hurting

He tends to them

Binds their wounds

As he kneels

Cares for them gently

As he deals

With a pain so profound

As he heals

Therapy.

He sits in a dimly lit room
The ceiling fan turns slowly above his head
Across from a total stranger
Expected to share
His thoughts and fears
Poker face is on
Clenching the arm of the chair
She starts asking questions
From superficial to deeply personal

The dam breaks
His heart aches
It's been aching
The river flows
Words spill out
Speaking of his lows
Speaking of the blows
As he hears himself talking he knows
Knows that once the dam is broken
It is almost impossible to be rebuilt
Now he is left vulnerable and open
But openness was the path to truth
Necessary to get to the root
The root of his problems
Needing to learn the cause to solve them

He spoke of losing loved ones in death
The crushing pain of a broken heart
Events not told in sequence
He didn't know where to start
Disappointments from friends
Many days being certain that it was the end
The end of his life
He needed a break
Yearned for an escape
From the prison of his mind
But he always came back
Thinking about his mother like a life line

How could he dream of hurting her?

She secretly became his hero
Even when he existed below zero
He thought about God
He thought about faith
Meditated on the truth
That if he was going through it
He could get through it

And that he was healing
Because he was *finally speaking*

The Recipe.

The recipe is simple. Gathering the ingredients from the soil however, can be hard. The love, it fuels our spirit and drives us forward. The faith, it infuses are blood with steel, constructs impenetrable towers in our hearts, making us untouchable, unbreakable. The hope, it designs and builds the most magnificent wings on our backs so that we can fly higher. Stir it up, slowly, let it marinate and come together within us. This is what freedom really tastes like.

Inheritance.

My reflection is no longer my enemy
I've learned to appreciate the melanin in my skin
To love the broadness of my nose
The fullness of my lips
The color of my dark brown eyes
It is my inheritance
Passed down to me by those before me
I have been learning
How to fall in love with it all

Called Its Name.

I pray in silence
And sit
I opened my mouth
And said it
In facing the beast
I found my release
Called its name
Without going insane
Admitted it to myself
Put pain on the shelf
Resisted the enemy
Dissolved the enmity
I needed to fight
To do what was right

Self-Worth.

He needed to
Once again

Believe in the light
That shined within.

Loveless.

He had to learn
To love himself again

It wasn't like
Riding a bike
It was a long
Tiring journey

Blowing off the cobweb
Pulling old memories
Of the shelf
Learning once again
How to love himself

Mothers Lesson.

She placed a voice in us
From as far back as we can remember
She taught us it was okay to express ourselves
To use our words even if it meant we didn't agree with her
She put to death the age old philosophy
That children are to be seen and not heard
She insisted on hearing us, She placed a voice in us
Drawing out what was in our hearts through questions
Teaching us to communicate through expression
She placed a voice in us, To speak up for what we know is wrong
To speak for those who didn't have a voice of their own
To speak when we were sad, to speak when we felt alone
She placed a voice in us, Helped us to realize that our feelings were valid
That they should be heard, She listened to every single word, She placed a voice in us.

Write.

Promise me
That every now and then
You will write love letters
To yourself

Promise

That you will practice
Being kind
Being patient
Loving yourself

Battle Ready.

He took his time

Carefully polished

His words

Like swords

He was a soldier

Going into battle

And he knew

He would need

Every weapon

At his disposal

Everyone Hurts.

When he gained the strength
To wipe the tears from his eyes
He could now see again
The space, this place around him
That everyone else was hurting as well

That this world was broken
That people with so little
Build so much after the fire
If only they have the desire

And he thought to himself
That maybe
Just maybe
That he too
Could possibly
Make it through

The Poison.

What they are offering you sweetly
Smoothly
With a soft voice
It's poisonous
As they try to convince you
That you are not enough

Whatever you do
Do not believe them
Do not consume it

These Words.

You'll need these words
In the future
As you have needed them
In the past

'Love Yourself
Always.'

Love is ... Part 2.

Love is found in actions
Silent countless expressions
Of affection

Wake up.

My dear
Please stop
Fooling yourself
A secret relationship
Is no
Relationship
At all

Little White Pill.

It's the way
His vision blurs
The image of people
Standing before him

The way their voices
Are drowned out

The gripping anxiety
As it surfaces
For no apparent reason
And that the voices
In his head
Get louder and louder

It's the feeling of guilt
As he looks down
At the little white pill
In the palm of his hand

It becomes his savior
The only thing
To quiet the voices
And pacify his guilt

For a moment
It takes away the feelings
By dulling his senses
Sinking his passions
Until he feels a little less

Because feeling less
Is better than feeling everything
All at once

The Scars.

The fire now torturing, burning
Becomes your refining
The weight woven within
The fabric of your being

The heaviness held on to
Builds strength
The tears that fall
Purifies your heart

The scars that cover your skin
Are now sacred symbols
Of wisdom

Her Hands.

His mother's hands
Those of a potter
Skillfully shaping
The clay spins
On the wheel
Making something real

Love guides her hands
As all good mothers are
She was an artist
And her son
A work of art
In her hands

Life Lesson 2.

Depression often hits in waves,

Sometimes lingering longer than we would like

Tugging at one's mind as they strive to get on with their daily lives

With that said, don't just wait it out

It is a force that must be faced head on

It must be met with everything positive and productive that we can think of

We must intentionally work at our healing

Surrounding ourselves with people and things that will pull us out of this quick sand

Depression is a war, so whatever you do, don't surrender

Chapter 3.

Coming Back Together.

He is back again
Not in the same way
He is different now
Stronger
Happier than before
The journey was hard
But he was gifted
With a reason to rise
He was gifted
With a reason to thrive

Hope.

Hopes warm light always shines
Sometimes as brightly as the sun
Other times a mere flicker in the dark
But it always shines
Inextinguishable
Illuminating the road before us

You Are.

Yes…

You are

Flawed

Yes…

You are

Beautiful

Bleeding.

Poets are the ones
Who allow themselves
To bleed onto paper
Converting their pain
Into art

Salamanca.

We were walking on cobblestone roads

Balconies of hanging plants above our heads

Arms out stretched

Fingers touching the stone walls beside us

Every street corner was a work of art
Thrown into the pages of a history book
Surrounded by massive ancient structures
From the breathtaking Plaza Mayor
To the ornate carvings on these historic buildings
Inhaling the foreign language surrounding me

The energy of the people
The richness of their culture
The smell of the food from the restaurants
As it lingers
In these streets
It's flavor as it lingers
on my tongue
Sangrias and tapas
Drinking wine as we sit in chairs on the sidewalk
As I put pen to paper
All these words fall out of me

This town is a perfect blend
Of brown sugar and cinnamon
It tastes so sweet and feels so warm
My once empty heart
Has been filled up
And it swells with gratitude
Changed my attitude
Like a different person in this place
Happiness was no longer something to chase
I possessed it in the palm of my hands
A realization of something I previously didn't understand
An emotional escape I didn't know I needed
Not until I finally received it
How is it that I could feel so at home
In a place so far from my own

Many Things.

He found that there's
No one immediate antidote to a broken heart

But that the cure was in several remedies

Gradually leading him

To the rediscovery of himself

Endurance.

The smell of the smoke remains
The scars and burns heal slowly
His lungs finally free again
Breathing in the air he had long forgotten
Then it hit him – he made it through
He made it to the other side of his personal storm
He gave up a million times in his head but never in his heart
He gave up on embracing happiness once more, gave up on hope
His heart however wouldn't allow him to let go
A flicker, a fire shined in the darkness
His fingers tightly clenched the slithers of light that remained
So he held on, endured the pain and persevered through the heat
He stood his ground, defying the tyranny of his own demons
He fought, he endured, he survived

Yellow Dress.

He remembers that day
Like it was yesterday
He heard the voice calling his name
From across the street
He looked over and there she was
Standing beautifully, radiantly
In the most delicate yellow dress
Waving at him
He doesn't recall walking over
All he knew was that in an instant
He was standing before her
Face to face

The only thing more dazzling
Than the sun was her smile

And even in that moment
He didn't know that this was
The beginning of the rest of his life

An Artist's Dream.

You are a literary masterpiece
Not a single chapter or book
You are an entire library
Filled with stories of incredible joy
And of unspeakable pain
Stories of how you defied the odds
And found love again

You are an artist's dream
Painted with every conceivable color
Of the most breathtaking sunset
The sun shines on you
Filters through you
It's light touches us
Blesses us
Impresses us
You have all my trust
Let's discuss

How beautiful you are
Shining in the darkness
Hung in the sky
The absolute brightest star

Dear Daddy.

I have a vision of you standing in a storm
It's dark, the winds are high and yet you stand
Allowing your faith to devour your fears
With an ability to see beyond the present
Staring at immortality from a distance
Or maybe it's not so distant
Perhaps it's right in front of you
I think that maybe you can you feel it

Touching the lives of many
Your actions build monuments of love in our hearts
Thank you for sewing compassion and empathy
Into the fabric of my being

A true spiritual soldier
Fewer men have ever been bolder

The Ones.

They are the ones
We wish were still with us

Spending their days on others
Placing hands in our chests
Pulling out buried potential
Raising us from the depths
Of our darkest insecurities
To breathe above the surface
Where the sun shines
Moving us by their lives

And if I'm making them
Sound perfect
I don't mean to

They had their flaws
Like the rest of us do
But somehow
They learned the secret
Of making broken
Unfold so beautifully

Have Faith.

Never forget
Faith isn't blind
Having eyes wide open
Anchored in truth
Shining light on the road
And providing the strength
To walk it again

When you have lost your way

Solemn.

It saddens me when I hear someone carelessly
Say of a poor soul who tragically
Took their own life
That it was cowardly
And selfish
Perhaps they have never experienced
A pain so profound that it cuts through you
Lacking the empathy needed to imagine a heart
On fire and then grounded into dust
It might just be genuine ignorance on their part
To a very real and dangerous condition

Or maybe they know all too well the hurt
Of drowning desperately into a sea of hopelessness and despair
Suffocating to the point where you pray for death
An escape from the stinging anxiety and feeling trapped
Within your own skin

Possibly they know it, lived it, it terrifies them
And instead of searching for help
They choose to hide these emotions

No matter the reason
It saddens me

Anchored.

It was his dreams
His hopes
His faith
His love
That kept him
From getting
Truly lost
Kept him
Grounded.

Warrior.

My heart reaches out to everyone who is hurting

I pray for all who feel alone
Who feel overcome by the darkness
Defeated by sadness

So please hear my words when I say
There is a warrior deep within you

Keep fighting for your happiness
Keep fighting for your life

Painted Hearts.
Three little flames
Dancing around
Souls blessed
Early lives
Filled with love
When he reunites
With his sisters
They sit down and reminisce
They speak of the small house
Making their mother miserable
As they ran around
They laughed
And played
And fought
And loved
And Cried
Memories they couldn't hide
Memories like colors
Painted on their hearts
The brightest most vibrant
Symbols of their childhood
When they were together
Speaking of old times
It felt good
Articulating dreams
Only they understood

Climbing on counter tops
To reach the highest shelf
Stealing out chocolates
Mother told them
They couldn't get
Running around the backyard
Sticking feathers in their hats
They could never sit and relax
Shared memories
Only they could reach

Now as adults
Keepers of their past
Holding the truth
That they are all they have

Love is …part 3.

That thing that follows you around
When you are trying to escape
It chases you down
Holds you by the shoulders
Looks you in the eye and says

*'I'm not leaving you
No matter how hard it gets'*

Born of Fire.

The greatest souls have never been crafted
By a life of ease

They are the ones who have
Intentionally built from their pain
They have taken the fire
That was burning them

And turned it into a tool of creation

Through Their Eyes.

If only you had the power
To see yourself as beautifully
As they see you

Love Letters.

His spoken word were both
Beautiful and true
But so often caught
In the passing wind

So he wrote letters
With indelible ink to signify
That his love for her
Would never ever die

Take time.

He didn't realize how much had changed
Until someone close to him said

"I've missed that sweet smile of yours."

Healing. Takes. Time

Paradise.

Take me to paradise
The grass is green and soft under our feet
It's the breezy part of the day
Singing black birds provide the music
For the children to dance and play
The shade hanging over our heads
Of the stately palm trees
We are conversing and laughing
Finally our hearts are freed

As we connect with friends and family
We speak of the struggles of our past
An untold suffering we swore would always last
But the past is the past
Our trials were really tests of which we passed

And now these stories feel so distant
We lie back on the grass
Can't shake the feeling, so reminiscent
It feels like someone else' story
We can no longer relate to the pain of our former selves
We are healed, we are whole again
And oh how it feels so nice
To be here together, standing in paradise

Love of my life.

Tell me how could one person be so strong
Inspiring me to believe in love again
With the warmth of her hands
The light of her smile
The compassion glowing from her heart
As we embark on a new journey
Getting lost in our own story
And in our truth
I'm learning that true love always
Presents powerful undeniable proof

He Uses Them.

At times
We receive
Minor divinities
In the kindness
Of others

Hearing God's voice
In the weight
Of their words

Why I Write.

Give me a cool Sunday
Pen in hand
Paper beneath it
Let me sit quietly and write all day

There is healing to be had through these words
Allow these sentiments to fly like birds

The way I write
Shaping these words in cursive
Aiming to be subversive
In overthrowing this pain
Self-worth is at stake
There is confidence to gain

The sound of the tip of my pen
As it glides across the pages
Calming the ocean inside
The sea that rages

Safe Space.

He was shattered internally when he met her again
She was so much light and warmth and truth
He could feel it coming from her
Without her saying a single word
He later learned why she was so wonderfully brilliant
You see, she had been refined by all of her challenges
She wore every scar and every line
Made it seem intentional
Used those long lessons
Learned how to walk with poise and grace
Chin lifted up by the inescapable truth
That she could never be replaced

It was that look on her face
That told him that he could be repaired
This thing between them was a safe space.

Becoming.

As the universe is expanding
Something in his heart
Was growing
He was in the process
Of becoming

And it was beautiful
So beautiful to watch

Renewed.

He is different now
Like he has lived
Ten lives before
He stands tall
Walks with a swagger
Speaks with confidence
He doesn't reside
In his own head
Not a diamond
In the rough
But refined
With so many stories
To tell
And it's amazing
To think
That the hurting
He prayed
To go away
Gave him
Wisdom
And strength
It paved the road
He now walked
With solid gold

Always With Us.

The days are not what we remember
The clouds have lifted
Clear blue skies
Bright brilliant Sun
Shining down on us
We smile more than we use to
Hearing the birds sing beautifully
We have each other
Standing here because
Of each other
Safe in the association
Of one another
Finally on the other side
Of the storm

Every now and then
When the laughter abates
His eyes glazed over
His mind drifted

Remembering those who
Were the foundation
Of our current prosperity
Chains not enslaving us
Tying us to our past
Even though they have past
The memory of them
It still lasts

The promise of being reunited
With them again
We trust
Now in our hearts
They are always with us

Ready.

Sitting back under a tree
Looking up at the clear blue sky
Gradually it came back to him
This excitement, a thirst for life
Thirst for association
Savoring these conversations

Now on a smoldering day
He was drinking a cold glass of lemonade
Lemonade made
From the high price paid
But he was smiling
He was hungry again
Hungry for education
Quiet and deep moments of meditation

He was ready to live once more
It was now his time to explore.

Head held high.

No one ever told you
That you were poured
From a golden cup

That there is
Royal blood
Running through
Your veins

And while they tell you
That you aren't better
Than anyone

Never forget
That no one is better
Than you

Trust me.

You will find love again

Or better yet

Love will find you again

The Result.

People looked up to him
Inspired by his words
Moved by his actions
Of kindness and compassion

What they didn't know
Was that he was the result

The result of the overcoming
Of darkness that tried
So desperately to drown him

Story-telling.

Only in telling his story
Did he realized
That he was never alone
That while the faces change
Within the shifting scenes
That he was connected
To the entire human family
Through the pain, the suffering
And through the healing

Breathless.

Every time she smiled
She took my breath away
And so I prayed to be breathless
All the days of my life

Inevitable.

Change is both
An uncomfortable
And necessary
Thing

Cliché.

And now
Because
Of her
He is
Full of
Clichés
Old love
Songs
And poetry

So much poetry

Gentle Rain

She has been
The gentle rain
Falling on
A cool day
While I sit
With a cup
Of hot
Chocolate
And a good
Book

She has been a blessing

The Power We Possess.

Human beings
Possess
The incredible
Ability
To will greatness
In Others

Focusing on them
Determined to pull
Their better selves
Out from within.

Mom&Dad.

And to my parents…
I have many heroes
Among which you
Are foremost

His World.

He recreated his own universe
Spread out a velvet sheet across
The sky
Carefully placing on it every star
Raising every sun and planet
Stirring every single solar system
slowly
Until it became what it was

Focusing on the gem
That caught his eye
He pours out an ocean over it
And shaped the hills and valleys
With his hands
He decorated the mountains
The beauty of these fountains
And he resided there
For many years
He lived in the world
That he created
With his own two hands

He was finally brave enough
To believe that he was enough

Brother.

An answer to a prayer
A prayer from a little boy
Who wanted more than anything
A younger brother
A best friend

Some people shift
The course of our lives
By simply being present
We become reminiscent
Of the moments shared
Two brothers dared
To embark on adventures
Traveling through worlds
Of absolute splendor

Forging a bond
That could never be broken
Communicating in ways
That remains unspoken

Where He Can Grow.

If you asked him where he got the inspiration for the stories he wrote
He'd tell you that sometimes he digs
Digs deep down into the dirty, dark, cold places, where fear and doubt resides

Sometimes however, he climbs, climbs mountains in order to feel the fresh breeze
That blows only at these
Heights and where the sun shines brightly, where he can touch the clouds of heaven

He would climb until he met a space of contentment and happiness
In short he goes where he can feel, he goes where he can learn, he goes where he can grow

Stubborn Creatures.

There are emotions
And feelings
And experiences
That cannot be
Put into words
No matter how hard
We try
It's like breathtaking landscapes
That no lens
Or paint brush
Could ever capture
All the colors
And countless shades
Within those colors
The unrehearsed movement
Of nature
The way the wind
Touches our skin
Carrying on its currents
Beautiful scents
Embracing our senses
The incredible experience
Of these scenes
It's found in what we feel
And what we feel
We can't explain
Even though it's so real

But writers and poets
Are such stubborn creatures
Relentless against all odds
In painting these pictures

Where She Lived.

He found her
In the stars

He was looking up
At the pitch black sky
It occurred to him
That one of his
Greatest blessings
Was standing right
In front of him

Beautiful Things.

Let me take a moment
And recognize the women
The pillars
Of my life

The lionesses who hunt
Who protect their young
Opening their hearts
To love fearlessly
Standing strong in
Their Sorrow tearless-ly

Their wisdom abounds
Compassion surrounds
Us
As we talk about them
Whether they be past or present
When they speak
Their voices roar
And rumbles through the grounds
Of our being
The ones responsible
For our seeing
The world through different eyes
It is truly no surprise
In the midst of adversity
That they choose to rise

The strength of their minds
Far exceeds their beauty
And man, aren't they
The most beautiful things you've ever seen
The heroes
Of this scene

When they walk
The earth moves
Defiantly speaking
To the world
Without a single word
Telling society
That "My value
Isn't determined by you"

I look up to them
Strong powerful women
Because they took control
Of their narrative
Wrote books and read
Their own story
Refusing to be put on the shelf
They insisted
On saving themselves

Life Lesson 3.

To be kind and forgiving doesn't mean allowing
Yourself to be taken advantage of
Understand that even more important
Than living with great compassion
Is possessing the wisdom to protect your heart
You must draw a line for those who may attempt
To abuse the valuable resource that is you
And then discard your friendship like it never mattered
Your ability and vast potential to help others
Is directly linked to how well you take care of yourself
Keeping your mental and emotional
Stability intact
Is absolutely essential

You Will.

Even if you break
Into a million pieces

You will

Come back together
You will always
Come back together

When I Am Weak.

Thank you for helping me
Find the strength in my
Vulnerability.

Greatness In You.

Borrow their eyes
If you have to
So that you
Could see
What they see in you

I won't tell you
A million more times
The exclusive place
You have in my mind

Or maybe the fact
That you fill up
My heart
And that for you
This is just the start

Perhaps I'll show
Spend all my days
Proving to you how much
You should be praised

Believing in you
Believing for you

Honesty.

Write it
How you feel it.

Unlocked Potential.

...And what if
You started believing in yourself again?

My Dear
You would be
A force
To be reckoned with

Harnessing.

Give yourself permission to feel everything in every way
The joy, the love, the anger, the fear – The heart stopping fear

Are all a part of life

It is okay to be open to feeling one or two or all of them all at once
This anxiety would break anyone unless it is harnessed and
embraced completely

Don't fight against the tide

Save your energy as you focus on the cause not the effect
Only then will it become your power
Even though you are far from perfect

Traveler.

You made it
Weary traveler
Drop your bags
Kick off your shoes
Fall back
Into the couch
By the door
Where the breeze is sweet
Drink something cold
And breathe in
The moment

You made it
Through
The wilderness
The long
Winding
Roads of loneliness
Under the navy blue
Velvet sky
When the stars
Didn't shine
As brightly
As they should have

Take it all in
Because you are here
Home at last my dear

Travel Often.

Be fearless
Go to places
That inspire you

Beyond words

The Old Me.

He found an old photograph of himself
Smiling but lost in the eyes
He didn't recognize this younger image of himself
He tucked it away safely in his wallet
A reminder of how far he had come

Prayer.

When we pray,
We rise

All Poets.

For some their poetry
Is written
For others their poetry
Is lived
Either way
In the end
We are all poets

God's Love.

Too many times
I failed to see God
When I was walking
In the dark
As he held my hand
Forgiving my ignorance
Gracing me with his love
Teaching me
Through the trials

Sometimes.

Sometimes we don't need answers
Sometimes there are no answers

We don't need a saving grace
Or a helping hand

Sometimes there are no wise words
No profound quotes

Sometimes all we need
Is peace and quiet

Learning How.

True happiness is an art form
A craft we spend our lives honing

Sunday Mornings.

The S – in Sunday
Is for Salvation
The salvation that comes
From the serenity
That centers you
Allowing you to reconnect
With yourself
For the spirituality
Raising your very being
Pushing you beyond
Your imperfections
That you may transcend
As you are reconnecting
With the Divine

Novel.

She is the most wonderful novel
I have ever read
From pages of sweet simplicity
Touching the depths of my heart
To the most profound thoughts
Feeding my mind

Dreamers.

Dreamers are always
The most vulnerable

Hearts on their sleeves
Emotions embroidered
On their skin
Vivid words describe
What they feel inside

Masks are foreign to them
Dreams inspired by freedom

Openness and honesty
The foundation
Of vulnerability

Vulnerability
The very essence
Of creativity

Perfect Distraction.

The ones who stay back
When the party is over
We linger
In the presence
Of one another
Our conversations
Laughing
Till our stomachs hurt
Bursting with joy
Tears of happiness
So distant
From the hurt
The jokes we tell
A perfect distraction
Saved by the purity
No sinking ships
Just the bliss
Of true friendships

Lingering.

Fear born
From the truth
That there is
No cure for
The darkness

That the voices
May always
Be there
Whispering
Terrible things
To you
About you

Courage is born
From the truth
That you have
Learned endurance
How to cope
To transform
The darkness
Into light

That now
You are a warrior
Fighting the voices
Casting them out
Calming the doubts

Gilded Cage.

She sits forward
Looks into his eyes
He told her all of his truth
Spoke of the unspeakable
Found illustrations
To help her see
Help her feel
The depth of his pain

She has no words

No wise words
Escape her lips
Her eyes project
Empathy
Her tears scream
Compassion

"I am grateful"
He says calmly
Consoling his confidant
"Life's war
Consistent battle
Has called from me
An internal renaissance
A relearning of myself
And what I believe
Forced to grow
Adjust my perspective
Forced essentially
Completely
To change
To transcend this
Gilded cage."

Because Of Them.

I've always been very protective
Of my siblings

I use to think that I had
To be strong for them
Now I know that I am strong
Because of them

Odyssey

The odyssey
Was a test

One of patience
Compassion
Faith
And love

So much love

Personal Revolution.

His revolution
Was quiet
Personal
And profound

Inspired.

Because of her
There is more
Poetry in my heart
Than I have time
To write

And that my dear
Is such a beautiful thing

Reclaiming.

In the end
Through
The ups
And downs
He became
A King
Reclaiming
His crown

In his mind

And that
Is all
That matters

Covenant.

Let's make a pact
And promise
That we will be
Kind to ourselves

Miserable & Magnificent.

He was mentored
And molded
By the unfolding
Of moments
Both miserable
And magnificent

New Music.

Now he has grown accustomed
To the music of healing
It is slow, it is smooth, it is silent
He gets lost in the sweet rhythm
Nothing like the sound of breaking
That once plagued him

He Picked Up The Pieces.

He collided with a force
Like a freight train
It moved through him
His heart shattered
Broken in two
Lying there helpless
Lost and hopeless
Many have been destroyed by far less
But there was something in him
It wouldn't allow him to rest
So he crawled painfully across the floor
Gathering the pieces
Like sharp shards of glass
That cut his hands
The individual pieces
Now scarlet stained
'He kept telling himself
This despair wouldn't last
If I keep going
The faster it will past'

He needs to face
All the different shapes
And shades of himself
From the brightest days of his heart
To the darkest corners of his soul

Eventually he picked up the pieces
He put back the puzzle of his own being
The picture was more beautiful
Than before the breaking
Even with the jagged lines running through
It was breath-taking

And now finally
Once more he was whole
Because from the moment he fell apart
This was his goal

Contents

Chapter 1, Shattered - 2.

Her Letters - 3.

I Feel You - 4.

He Has To - 5.

Don't Cry - 6.

Mental Illness - 7.

Known As - 8.

The Privilege of Pain - 9.

Sacred Tears - 10.

Wrong For Each Other - 11.

Mother's foresight - 12.

Mid-night Prayers - 13.

The Left Side - 14.

Dearly Beloved - 15.

Missing Her - 16.

Guilty - 17.

Beautiful Hearts - 18.

The Weight - 19.

Begin Somewhere - 20.

Broken Things Breaking Things - 21.

Depression - 22.

The Way it is - 23.

Unheard - 24.

He Waits - 25.

We All Break - 26.

Never Forget - 27.

Love is… Part 1 - 28.

Numb - 29.

I Am Here - 30.

Life Lesson 1 - 31.

Chapter 2, Picking Up The Pieces - 32.

The Center - 33.

Culture of Silence - 34.

Mortality - 35.

It is Sacred - 36.

A Mother's Love - 37.

12:45 - 38.

The Apology - 39.

My Father would say - 40.

Change - 41.

For Them - 42.

Therapy - 43.

The Recipe - 45.

Inheritance - 46.

Called its name - 47.

Self-Worth - 48.

Loveless - 49.

Mother's Lesson - 50.

Write - 51.

Battle Ready - 52.

Everyone Hurts - 53.
The Poison - 54.
These Words - 55.
Love is … Part 2 - 56.
Wake up - 57.
Little White Pill - 58.
The Scars - 59.
Her Hands - 60.
Life Lesson 2 - 61.

Chapter 3, Coming Back Together - 62.

Hope - 63.
You Are - 64.
Bleeding - 65.
Salamanca - 66.
Many Things - 68.
Endurance - 69.
Yellow Dress - 70.
An Artist's Dream - 71.
Dear Daddy - 72.
The Ones - 73.
Have Faith - 74.
Solemn - 75.
Anchored - 76.
Warrior - 77.

Painted Hearts - 78.
Love is …part 3 - 79.
Born of Fire - 80.
Through Their Eyes - 81.
Love Letters - 82.
Take time - 83.
Paradise - 84.
Love of my life - 85.
He uses them - 86.
Why I write - 87.
Safe Space - 88.
Becoming - 89.
Renewed - 90.
Always With Us - 91.
Ready - 92.
Head held high - 93.
Trust me - 94.
The Result - 95.
Story-telling - 96.
Breathless - 97.
Inevitable - 98.
Cliché - 99.
Gentle Rain - 100.
The Power We Possess - 101.
Mom&Dad - 102.
His World - 103.

Brother - 104.
Where He Can Grow - 105.
Stubborn Creatures - 106.
Where She Lived - 107.
Beautiful Things - 108.
Life Lesson 3 - 110.
You Will - 111.
When I am weak - 112.
Greatness In You - 113.
Honesty - 114.
Unlocked Potential - 115.
Harnessing - 116.
Traveler - 117.
Travel Often - 118.
The Old Me - 119.
Prayer - 120.
All Poets - 121.
God's Love - 122.
Sometimes - 123.
Learning How - 124.
Sunday Mornings - 125.
Novel - 126.
Dreamers - 127.
Perfect Distraction - 128.
Lingering - 129.
Gilded Cage - 130.
Because of Them – 131.
Odyssey - 132.
Personal Revolution - 133.
Inspired - 134.
Reclaiming - 135.
Covenant - 136.
Miserable & Magnificent - 137.
New Music - 138.
He Picked Up The Pieces - 139.

Manufactured by Amazon.ca
Bolton, ON